max science primary

Journal 5

DISCOVERING THROUGH ENQUIRY

LAWRIE RYAN

SERIES EDITOR: **BOB KIBBLE**

macmillan education

INTERNATIONAL CURRICULUM

Macmillan Education
4 Crinan Street
London N1 9XW
A division of Springer Nature Limited

Companies and representatives throughout the world

Journal ISBN 978-1-380-02169-4

First published 2019

Original design by EMC Design Ltd and Macmillan Education
Page make-up by Ink Design
IIllustrated by Sandy Lightely, Martin Cain and Ilias Arahovitis c/o Beehive Illustration Agency, Sandy Lightely pp 1, 2, 3, 9 (bottom), 12, 17, 18, 22, 23, 27, 33, 34, 35, 38, 39, 43, 44, 45, 49, 55, 58, 61, 62, 66, 68, 71, 76, 78, 81, 82, 86, 87, 91, 93, 96, 97, 98; Martin Cain c/o Beehive Illustration pp 8; Ilias Arahovitis c/o Beehive Illustration pp 9 (top)
Cover design by Sparks Publishing Services Ltd and Macmillan Education
Cover illustration by Star Publishing Pte Ltd and Jorge Santillan c/o Beehive Illustration Agency

Printed and bound in Spain
2023 2022 2021 2020 2019
10 9 8 7 6 5 4 3 2 1

Contents

Introducing the *Max Science primary* Journal

The ***Max Science primary* Journal** complements the ***Max Science primary*** series by providing a link between learning at school and learning at home. It matches the topics from the course and the Cambridge Primary Science Curriculum framework with a topic-by-topic series of structured activities for learners to complete with an adult.

As a parent or carer, it is sometimes difficult to know what is being taught in school and how your child is really doing in a subject. Do they enjoy it? Do they understand the concepts and the vocabulary? This Journal lets you spend time together at home in a supportive way and find out how they are doing in science.

Introducing the topic

A cartoon image and question introduce every science topic in a fun and engaging way.

1 Ourselves

1.1 The human body

Some things the same, some things different

Humans are not exactly the same as one another either. We have differences that allow us to tell one another apart.

Look at the cartoon.

Both children have a head.

What other things can you see that are the same?

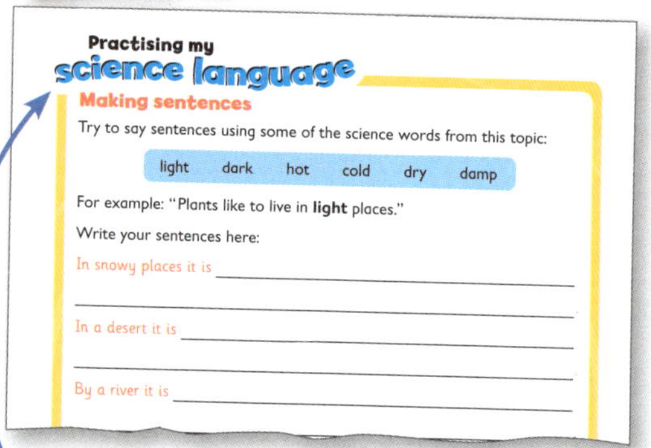
Practising my science language

Making sentences

Try to say sentences using some of the science words from this topic:

light dark hot cold dry damp

For example: "Plants like to live in **light** places."

Write your sentences here:

In snowy places it is ____

In a desert it is ____

By a river it is ____

Practising my science language

This feature allows learners to practise using key words to improve scientific vocabulary and to make it easier to learn science in English.

Check my science

Each topic allows learners to check their understanding through this activity.

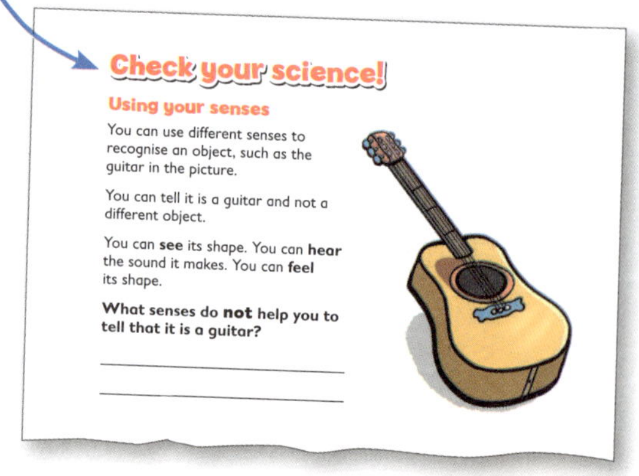
Check your science!

Using your senses

You can use different senses to recognise an object, such as the guitar in the picture.

You can tell it is a guitar and not a different object.

You can **see** its shape. You can **hear** the sound it makes. You can **feel** its shape.

What senses do **not** help you to tell that it is a guitar?

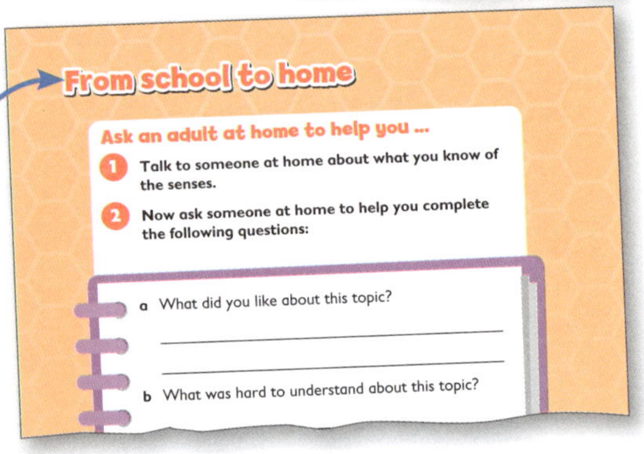
From school to home

Ask an adult at home to help you ...

1 Talk to someone at home about what you know of the senses.

2 Now ask someone at home to help you complete the following questions:

a What did you like about this topic?

b What was hard to understand about this topic?

From school to home

You can work together at home to complete this section at the end of each topic. The Journal can then be taken into school for the teacher to look at and discuss, and acts as a record of the learners' progress.

1 The way we see things

1.1 Sources of light and seeing

In Topic 1.1, you should be able to list some light sources and describe how we can see them. You should be able to show this on diagrams by drawing rays of light travelling in straight lines.

You should also be able to explain how shadows are formed.

Look at this football stadium lit up for a match at night.

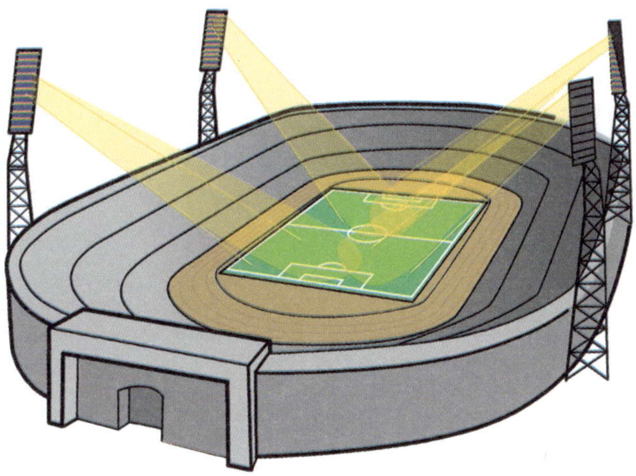

1. **What are the light sources?** ______________________________

2. **How many shadows would a player standing in the middle of the pitch have?** ______________________________

3. **Explain why this is.**

____

____

____

____

Look at these two cars on a misty night.

Dipped beam

Full beam

1. **What is the light source in the pictures?** ____________________

2. **Why do cars have two settings for their headlights?**

   You can ask someone at home to help you answer this question.

   ____

   ____

   ____

   ____

Check your science!

1. List four light sources.

2. Amira is reading her book at night.

   a) Draw a light ray on the picture to show how Amira can see the words and pictures in the book.

   Use a ruler to draw the light ray.

   Remember to use an arrowhead on the light ray to show the direction the light travels in.

   b) i) Where would Amira's shadow be?

   ii) Explain why Amira forms a shadow.

3. Objects can be transparent, translucent or opaque.

   Explain the differences between these three words.

Practising my

science language

1. Try to complete this crossword.

Across

5. Light has been blocked here behind an object.
6. A ray __________ shows the path of light on a science drawing.
7. This word describes an object that some light can pass through.
8. This word describes the light coming from a torch – a __________ of light.

Down

1. This word describes an object that light passes straight through.
2. Light travels in __________ lines.
3. This is a line that shows the path of light on a science drawing.
4. This word describes an object that no light passes through.

2. Show your crossword to someone at home.

Cover the crossword and see if they can answer any of the clues.

Can they find any answers that you could not?

From school to home

Ask an adult at home to help you ...

1. **Talk to an adult about what you know about sources of light, how we see light and how shadows are formed. Practise saying the key words. Say the key words in sentences.**

2. **Now ask someone at home to help you complete the following questions.**

a What did you like about this topic?

____

____

____

b What was hard to understand about this topic?

____

____

____

I understand. | I understand a bit. | I need more time to understand this.

3 **Now look at the checklist below. How are you doing? Circle one face for each statement.**

- I know some light sources.
- I know how we can see a light source.
- I can explain how shadows are formed.
- I know that light travels in straight lines.
- I can draw rays of light on a ray diagram.

4 **Ask an adult at home to read and sign this.**

I have checked learning on this topic.

We have shared some understanding at home.

Signed: ______________________

Date: ______________

Teacher comment: ______________________________

____

Date: ______________

1.2 Mirrors and light investigations

In Topic 1.2, you should be able to show how rays of light can be reflected by surfaces, describe some uses of mirrors and explain what makes a good reflector of light.

You should also be able to investigate the brightness of light and its reflection.

Look at the orange car. It is trying to turn on to a busy road. We are looking down onto the car from above the road.

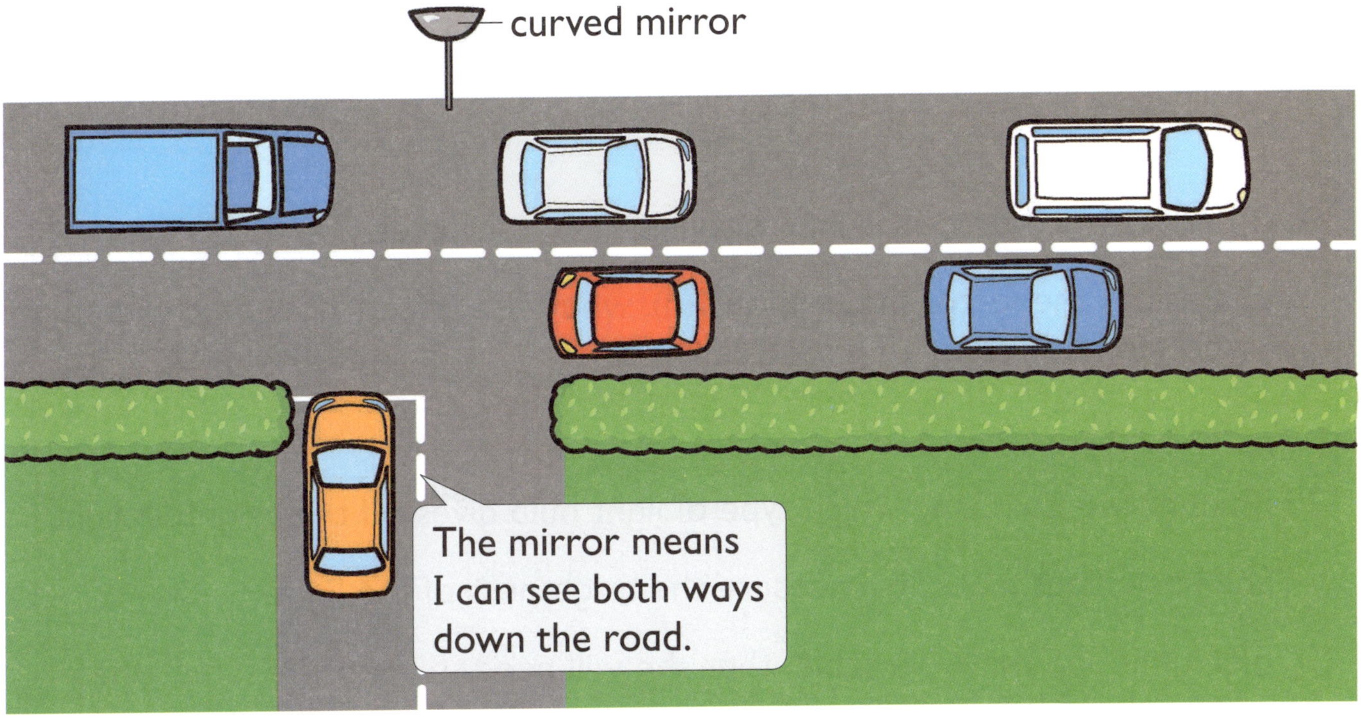

1. **Explain how the curved mirror makes the road a safer place than before.**

____

____

2. **Show your answer to someone at home who can drive. How else can we use mirrors to make cars safer?**

____

____

Check your science!

1. **a)** Complete the diagram to show what happens to light rays as they bounce off:

   i) a smooth surface

   ii) a rough surface.

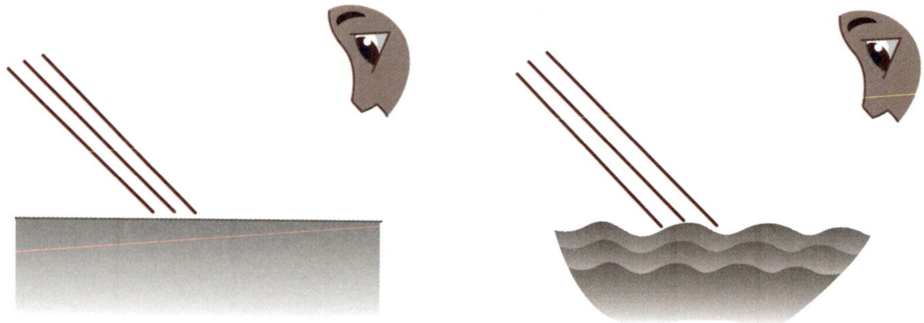

   b) What word describes light bouncing off a surface? ____________________

   c) Besides the factor in question 1(a), what else affects how much light can be seen bouncing off a surface?

   ____

2. Rhianna wants to see which type of light bulb gives off the brightest light.

   She has a light meter to measure the brightness of the light.

   a) Name one thing (variable) that she will need to keep the same when testing each light bulb.

   ____

   b) Why does Rhianna have to keep the answer to question 2(a) the same?

   ____

   c) Rhianna decides to test each light bulb three times. Why does she repeat each test?

   ____

   d) Write down one use of light meters.

   ____

Practising my

science language

1. Fill in the missing letters to complete these sentences. The first letter of each missing word is given:

   a) To be a good reflector of light, a surface needs to be both s _ _ _ _ and s _ _ _ _ _.

   b) Poor reflectors of light have d _ _ _ and r_ _ _ _ _ surfaces.

2. These two students are testing which materials are the best reflectors of light.

   Fill in the missing words to complete these sentences:

   a) The ruler is used to make sure that it is a _ _ _ _ _ _ _ _.

   b) At first the students just used their eyes to judge the brightness of the light. Then they used a _ _ _ _ _ _ _ _ _ _ _ _ to make their results more reliable.

   c) At the end of their investigation, they wrote down the order of the materials in their _ _ _ _ _ _ _ _ _ _ _ _ _ _.

3. Complete and label the diagram showing the reflection of light from a mirror.

From school to home

Ask an adult at home to help you ...

1. Talk to an adult about what you know about how rays of light are reflected from surfaces, and about mirrors. Practise saying the key words. Say the key words in sentences.

2. Now ask someone at home to help you complete the following questions.

a What did you like about this topic?

___

___

___

b What was hard to understand about this topic?

___

___

___

I understand. I understand a bit. I need more time to understand this.

3 **Now look at the checklist below. How are you doing? Circle one face for each statement.**

- I can show how rays of light can be reflected by surfaces.
- I know how we can see a reflection of an object.
- I can describe some uses of mirrors.
- I can describe and explain what makes a good reflector of light.
- I can investigate the brightness of light and its reflection.

4 **Ask an adult at home to read and sign this.**

I have checked learning on this topic.

We have shared some understanding at home.

Signed: ______________________

Date: ______________

Teacher comment: ______________________________

____

Date: ______________

2 Evaporation and condensation

2.1 Evaporation and condensation in everyday life

In Topic 2.1, you should know what "evaporation" and "condensation" mean and be able to give some examples of each process.

You should also be able to describe what happens to the particles in a liquid when it evaporates, and what happens to the particles in a gas when it condenses.

Picture A

Picture B

Hiro and Tami are helping to hang out the washing to dry.

1. a) Will the washing dry faster in picture A or B? ________________

b) List three reasons why.

i) ________________________________

ii) ________________________________

iii) ________________________________

2. Write a note to Hiro and Tami giving them tips on when and how to hang the washing out to dry it as quickly as possible. Include the word "evaporate".

____

____

____

Check your science!

1. Fill in the missing letters to complete these sentences. The first letter of each missing word is given:

a) When a material evaporates there is a change of s _ _ _ _.

b) In this process a l _ _ _ _ _ changes into a g _ _.

c) Particles escape from the s _ _ _ _ _ _ and mix with the particles of a _ _ above the liquid.

d) When a gas turns into a liquid, we say that the gas has c _ _ _ _ _ _ _ _.

e) This happens when the temperature gets c _ _ _ _ _.

f) The particles in gas get c _ _ _ _ _ together as it turns into liquid.

2. Decide whether each statement is an example of condensation or evaporation. Tick the correct box.

a) A puddle dries up in the playground at school.

Condensation ☐ **Evaporation** ☐

b) You can smell fresh bread baking throughout your home.

Condensation ☐ **Evaporation** ☐

c) The mirror mists up in the bathroom.

Condensation ☐ **Evaporation** ☐

d) Clouds form in the sky as the temperature of water vapour decreases.

Condensation ☐ **Evaporation** ☐

3. A bottle of perfume is left on a sunny windowsill with its top off. An identical bottle containing the same amount of perfume is also left with its top off but it is placed inside a cupboard.

a) Predict what will happen.

I think that ____

____.

b) Explain why this is. Mention the "particles" of perfume.

Because ____

____.

Practising my science language

1. Label each arrow between the two boxes:

2. Rearrange the letters in each box to give the name of a liquid or a gas at room temperature.

   Circle "liquid" or "gas" to show the correct state.

   a) | r e l p o t | _ _ _ _ _ _ is a **liquid / gas**.

   b) | m a s e t | _ _ _ _ _ is a **liquid / gas**.

   c) | l o i | _ _ _ is a **liquid / gas**.

3. Imagine that you are a particle of water coming out of the hot tap into a steaming bath of water. You end up in a drop of cold water on the bathroom mirror.

   a) Write a paragraph about what happens to you and your particle friends on your journey from tap to mirror.

   b) Read your story to someone at home. Answer any questions they have.

From school to home

Ask an adult at home to help you ...

1. Talk to an adult about what you know about evaporation and condensation. Practise saying the key words. Say the key words in sentences.
2. Now ask someone at home to help you complete the following questions.

a What did you like about this topic?

____

____

____

b What was hard to understand about this topic?

____

____

____

I understand. I understand a bit. I need more time to understand this.

3 Now look at the checklist below. How are you doing? Circle one face for each statement.

- I can describe what "evaporation" and "condensation" mean.
- I can list some examples of evaporation and condensation.
- I can describe what happens to the particles in a liquid when it evaporates.
- I can investigate and understand what affects the drying of clothes on a washing line.
- I can describe what happens to the particles in a gas when the gas condenses.

4 Ask an adult at home to read and sign this.

I have checked learning on this topic.

We have shared some understanding at home.

Signed: ______________________

Date: ______________

Teacher comment: ______________________________

____

Date: ______________

2.2 The water cycle

In Topic 2.2, you should be able to describe the water cycle that occurs in nature and explain its stages, including any changes of state.

You should also be able to explain the water cycle using the idea of water particles.

You cannot run through a **solid** wall.

You can run through **liquid** water, but it is hard work!

It is easy to run through air, which is a mixture of **gases**.

Explain to someone at home what is happening in each picture.

Check your science!

1. Fill in the missing changes of state:

   a) When a ______________ condenses, it becomes a liquid.

   b) When a ______________ evaporates, it becomes a gas.

2. Put these ten events in the water cycle into the correct order, from 1 to 10.

   The first and last steps have been done for you.

1	Energy from the Sun warms up the sea.
	The tiny water droplets form clouds.
	Water evaporates from seawater.
	As the clouds rise over the land, the tiny droplets of water get bigger.
	The liquid water goes back to the sea in streams and rivers.
	Water rises above the sea as water vapour.
	The water vapour gets cooler as it rises and condenses to form small droplets of liquid water.
	When the drops of water are heavy enough, they fall to the ground as rain.
	The wind blows the clouds over the land.
10	Then the water cycle starts all over again.

3. Dewain and Melissa each have an idea about the particles that make up water.

Who has the right idea? ______________

Practising my

science language

1. Fill in the missing words to complete this description of the water cycle. Use the words from the box:

melts	rain	colder	rivers	Sun	evaporates	wind
condenses	sea	freeze	vapour	snow	rise	warm

Energy from the _________ heats the sea. This _________ water from seawater. The water rises into the air as water _________.

The air gets _________ the higher up you go. Clouds start to form when the water vapour _________ as small droplets of liquid water.

The _________ blows the clouds over the land. As the clouds _________ the tiny droplets of water join together. When the bigger drops are heavy enough, they fall to the ground as _________.

Some clouds get blown over mountains. This can make the air so cold that the water droplets _________ to form tiny ice crystals in the clouds. Again, when heavy enough they fall towards the ground. If the air below is _________ enough, the ice _________ and we get rain. If the air below the cloud is cold enough, the ice crystals fall to the ground as _________.

Streams and _________ return the liquid water to the _________ for the cycle to begin again.

2. a) Draw a cartoon strip showing the adventures of a water particle as it travels from the sea to a cloud, and then falls in a raindrop. Be creative!

   b) Show your cartoon strip to someone at home. Explain it to them and answer any questions they have.

From school to home

Ask an adult at home to help you ...

1. **Talk to an adult about what you know about the water cycle. Practise saying the key words. Say the key words in sentences.**

2. **Now ask someone at home to help you complete the following questions.**

a What did you like about this topic?

____

____

____

b What was hard to understand about this topic?

____

____

____

I understand. I understand a bit. I need more time to understand this.

3 **Now look at the checklist below. How are you doing? Circle one face for each statement.**

- I can describe the water cycle that occurs in nature.
- I can explain the stages of the water cycle, including any changes of state.
- I can use the idea of water particles when explaining the water cycle.

4 **Ask an adult at home to read and sign this.**

I have checked learning on this topic.

We have shared some understanding at home.

Signed: ______________________

Date: ______________

Teacher comment: ______________________________

____

Date: ______________

2.3 Changing the state of water

In Topic 2.3, you should be able to tell the difference between boiling and evaporation. You should also know the melting point and the boiling point of water.

Kassim is having some trouble with his mum, dad and sister – but his little brother catches him out!

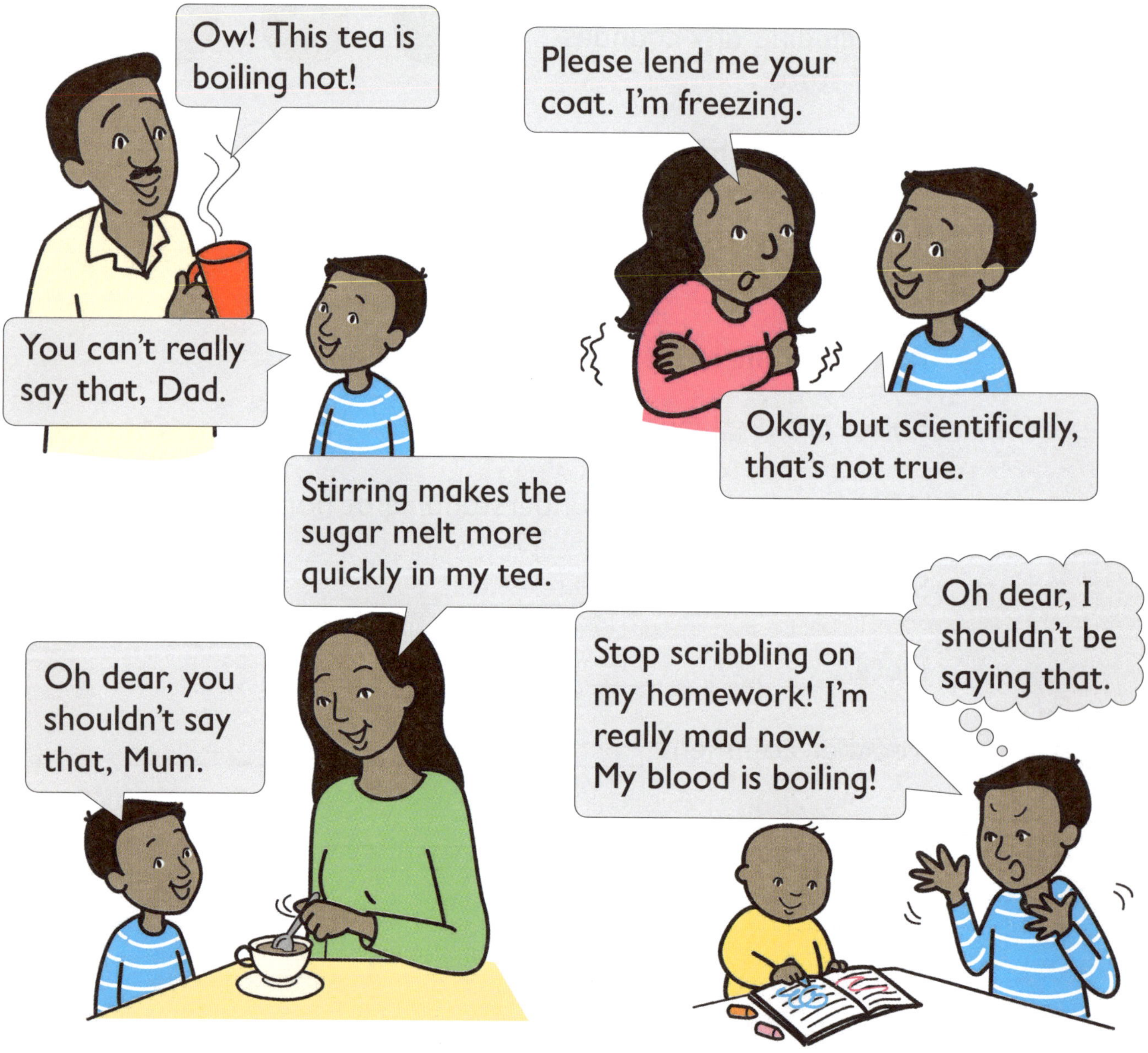

Explain to someone at home how these everyday uses of "changes of state" words are not scientifically correct.

Check your science!

1. Fill in the missing changes of state.

ice ← ________ water ← ________ steam

(ice ________ → water ________ → steam)

2. Fill in the missing words to complete these sentences. Use the words from the box:

ice water steam

a) You cannot change the shape of ________ without smashing it.

b) The particles can slip and slide over each other in ________.

c) ________ can be poured into an open container and will stay there.

d) ________ fills its whole container.

e) The particles are tightly packed in ________.

f) The particles are widely spaced in ________.

g) You can only squash ________.

h) The particles are fixed in position but can vibrate in ________.

3. Look at the sketch graph showing what happens when water is heated in a kettle.

Describe what happens to the line on the graph when the water starts to boil.

____

____

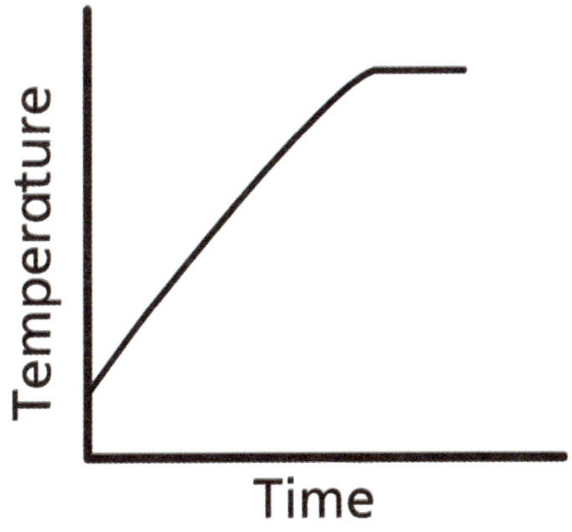

Practising my science language

1. Rearrange the letters in the boxes to find two measuring instruments you could use to measure the boiling point of water.

t o e m e h r e m t r

t _ _ _ _ _ _ _ _ _ _

t m r e a r t u e p e	s n e o s r

t _ _ _ _ _ _ _ _ _ _   **s** _ _ _ _ _

2. Tick the unit we use for temperatures.

☐ **kg**   ☐ **m**   ☐ **°C**

3. Tick the correct word to finish the sentence.

When a gas escapes from the surface of a liquid below its boiling point, we call the process ...

☐ **evaporation**   ☐ **boiling**

☐ **melting**   ☐ **condensation**

4. Label the "melting point" and the "boiling point" of water on the temperature line.

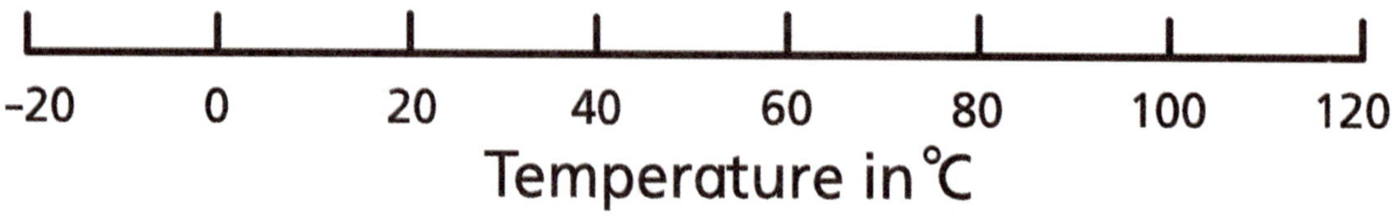

From school to home

Ask an adult at home to help you ...

1. Talk to an adult about what you know about boiling, and the melting and boiling points of water. Practise saying the key words. Say the key words in sentences.

2. Now ask someone at home to help you complete the following questions.

a What did you like about this topic?

____

____

____

b What was hard to understand about this topic?

____

____

____

I understand. I understand a bit. I need more time to understand this.

3 **Now look at the checklist below. How are you doing? Circle one face for each statement.**

- I can tell the difference between boiling and evaporation.
- I know the melting point of water.
- I know the boiling point of water.

4 **Ask an adult at home to read and sign this.**

I have checked learning on this topic.

We have shared some understanding at home.

Signed: ______________________________

Date: __________________

Teacher comment: ____

____

Date: __________________

2.4 Making and separating solutions

In Topic 2.4, you should be able to test whether materials are soluble or insoluble. You should be able to separate a mixture of materials by sieving or filtering.

You should also be able to collect a solid from a solution.

1. **Explain to Tarla's dad what happens when he filters his coffee.**

____

____

2. **Explain to Tarla's mum what happens when she dissolves jelly cubes in hot water.**

____

____

Check your science!

1. Narin wants to separate a mixture of sand and water.

   She decides to filter the mixture.

   Draw a labelled diagram of the apparatus she could use.

2. Grains of sand are larger than the grains of iron in iron filings.

   What method can you use to separate these two insoluble materials?

   ____

3. In hot countries, you can collect sea salt from seawater.

   The seawater runs into wide, shallow areas called salt pans. It is left until the solid sea salt can be scraped up and collected.

   a) Name the change of state that takes place. ______________________________

   b) Why are the salt pans wide and shallow?

   ____

   ____

Practising my science language

1. Bastian makes a sweet cup of tea for his mum, but she does not like sugar!

   He has a bright idea: he will filter the tea using the paper in the coffee maker.

   a) What happens when Bastian tries filtering the sweet tea?

   Tick the correct answer.

   - ☐ The sweet tea stays in the filter funnel.
   - ☐ The sugar goes through the filter paper.
   - ☐ The sugar is left behind in the filter paper.

   b) Tick the correct ending for the sentence.

   This happens because ...

   - ☐ ... all the sweet tea in the cup is soaked up by the filter paper.
   - ☐ ... the sugar is a solid so it cannot get through the tiny holes in the filter paper.
   - ☐ ... the sugar breaks up into really small particles as it dissolves in the hot tea – these particles can pass through the tiny holes in the filter paper.

Practising my

science language

2. Find these words in the wordsearch.

dissolve soluble solution insoluble solid

particles sieve filter evaporate

a	t	b	y	a	w	e	f	a	w	m	c	f	f	y
d	t	g	n	t	r	v	i	u	x	e	e	r	z	u
v	c	t	l	i	q	a	q	b	e	r	i	d	e	b
w	z	n	r	z	k	p	a	r	t	i	c	l	e	s
s	u	j	t	r	z	o	t	s	o	l	i	d	t	c
i	t	s	b	g	h	r	f	s	a	f	c	r	i	v
e	s	h	r	n	n	a	i	g	t	v	y	o	r	q
v	k	s	e	h	r	t	l	e	k	d	i	y	o	s
e	l	o	m	c	q	e	t	r	e	z	z	v	c	o
l	b	l	f	y	i	k	e	d	m	e	k	z	t	l
t	d	u	o	w	l	b	r	y	s	l	q	h	t	u
a	h	t	d	i	s	s	o	l	v	e	u	h	s	b
d	e	i	n	s	o	l	u	b	l	e	k	l	s	l
e	g	o	a	o	l	e	s	e	a	g	p	f	z	e
t	v	n	x	q	k	p	c	u	y	t	t	a	l	s

From school to home

Ask an adult at home to help you ...

1. Talk to an adult about what you know about making and separating solutions. Practise saying the key words. Say the key words in sentences.

2. Now ask someone at home to help you complete the following questions.

a What did you like about this topic?

____

____

____

b What was hard to understand about this topic?

____

____

____

I understand. I understand a bit. I need more time to understand this.

3 **Now look at the checklist below. How are you doing? Circle one face for each statement.**

- I can test whether materials are soluble or insoluble.
- I know how to separate a mixture of materials by sieving.
- I know how to separate a mixture of materials by filtering.
- I can describe how to collect a solid from a solution.

4 **Ask an adult at home to read and sign this.**

I have checked learning on this topic.

We have shared some understanding at home.

Signed: ______________________

Date: ______________

Teacher comment: ______________________________

____

Date: ______________

3 The life cycle of a flowering plant

3.1 Monitoring plant growth

In Topic 3.1, you should be able to monitor changes in plant growth over time. You should also be able to describe how to record and display data over time.

Kiri and Azumi are thinking about how they have developed their skills in observing and measuring data since starting school.

When we first observed plants, we talked about how they 'got bigger', got 'more leaves' and 'grew into pretty flowers' when we looked after them for a few weeks.

1, 2, 3, 4, 5 leaves. Now let's count the petals on the flowers.

We can then draw a graph to show the pattern over time.

Now we can measure changes carefully as a plant grows, and record the data in a table we design ourselves.

1. **How do your skills in observing and measuring change as you get older? Think of three things.**

   a) ______________________________

   b) ______________________________

   c) ______________________________

2. **Explain to someone at home how your science skills in observing and measuring have improved since you started school.**

   Give them some examples from this year's work.

Check your science!

1. Use your ruler to measure the height of this seedling as it changes over time.

After 2 days | After 4 days | After 6 days | After 8 days

2. a) Complete the headings in the table.

Time in ______________	______________ of seedling in cm

b) Fill in the table using your measurements from question 1.

3. What type of graph would you draw to display the results from the table?

☐ **Bar chart**

☐ **Line graph**

Practising my science language

1. Binita is growing a plant. She decides to give the plant 5 cm³ of water each day.

a) Fill in the missing letters to describe how Binita will measure the volume of water. The first letter of each missing word is given. Some of the gaps need to be filled with numbers:

Binita will use a small m _ _ _ _ _ _ _ _ cylinder to get exactly _____ cm³ of w _ _ _ _. She will make sure her eye is l _ _ _ _ with the mark for number _____ on the scale.

Then she will carefully p _ _ _ water into the measuring cylinder until the b _ _ _ _ _ _ of the curve is level with the mark exactly between _____ cm³ and _____ cm³.

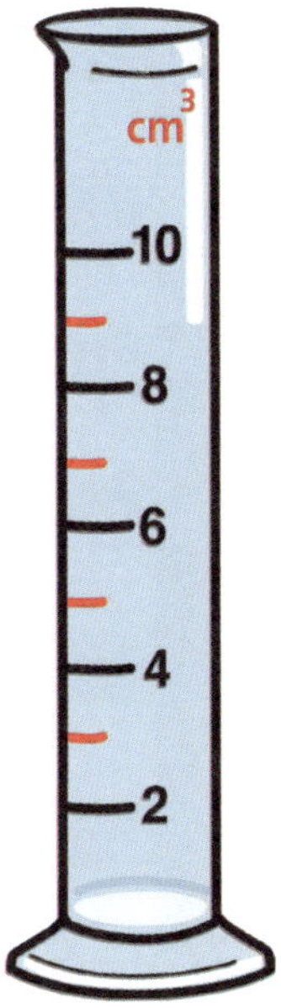

b) Draw in the level of the water that Binita will add each day. Remember that the surface of the water will be slightly curved.

2. Scientists often record the results of their investigations in tables. This is the top of a table of results:

Time in days	Mass of bean in g

a) Fill in the missing letters to describe how most tables are drawn. The first and last letters of each word are given:

The top line of a table contains the h _ _ _ _ _ _ s.
If measurements are recorded the u _ _ _ s are included.
Under these, there are horizontal r _ _ s. Tables are also divided into vertical c _ _ _ _ _ s.

b) Fill in the missing letters to complete the question the scientists who drew this table were investigating. The first letter of each missing word is given:

How does the m _ _ _ of a b _ _ _ change over t _ _ _?

From school to home

Ask an adult at home to help you ...

1. Talk to an adult about what you know about how to monitor and record changes in plant growth over time. Practise saying the key words. Say the key words in sentences.

2. Now ask someone at home to help you complete the following questions.

a What did you like about this topic?

____

____

____

b What was hard to understand about this topic?

____

____

____

I understand. I understand a bit. I need more time to understand this.

3 **Now look at the checklist below. How are you doing? Circle one face for each statement.**

- I can observe and measure changes in plant growth over time.
- I know how to record and display data about plant growth over time.

4 **Ask an adult at home to read and sign this.**

I have checked learning on this topic.

We have shared some understanding at home.

Signed: ____________________

Date: ____________

Teacher comment: ____________________________

____

Date: ____________

3.2 Seed dispersal

In Topic 3.2, you should be able to understand why plants disperse their seeds and the different ways they can do this.

You should also be able to identify germination as the process following seed dispersal.

Look at this cartoon of Pilot Sam's day. Sam is a seed.

1

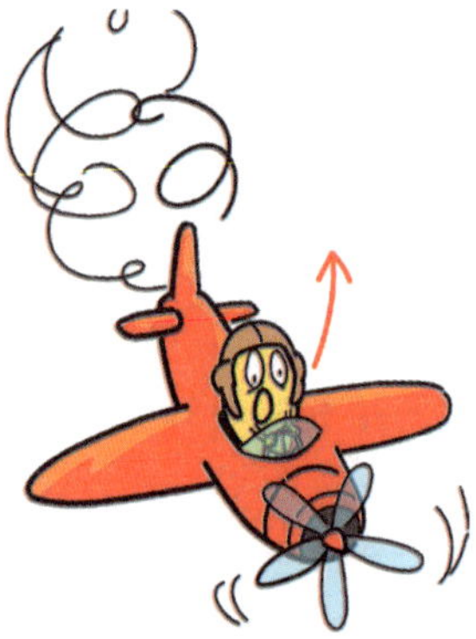

Sam has to press the ejector button in his aeroplane.

2

Sam's parachute opens.

3

Sam lands in a lake and has to swim ashore.

4

He hitches a ride home on a horse's back.

1. **Explain how Pilot Sam's unfortunate day could be used to model four different ways in which plants spread their seeds.**

   a) ______________________________

   b) ______________________________

   c) ______________________________

   d) ______________________________

2. **Explain to someone at home how the cartoon links to seed dispersal.**

Check your science!

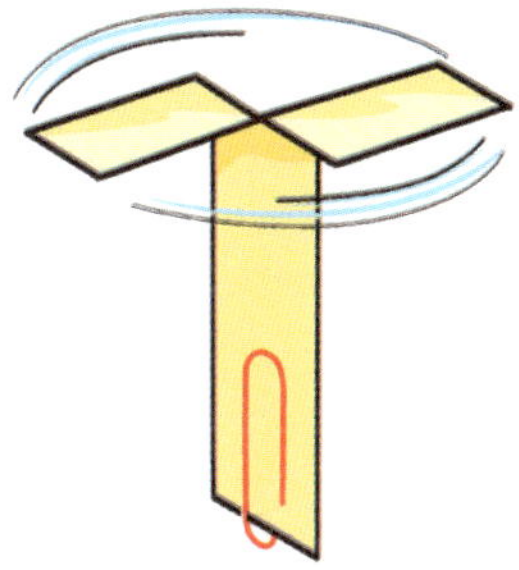

Some learners are investigating how to use paper spinners to model seed dispersal from a maple tree.

They decide to see if the length of the spinner's wings affects how long it takes to fall. They repeat each test three times.

1. To complete the results table, work out the average (mean) time when the wings are 5 cm long. Add up the 1st, 2nd and 3rd tries in the bottom row of the table. Then divide your answer by 3.

Length of wings in cm	Time for paper spinner to hit the floor in seconds			
	1st try	2nd try	3rd try	Average (mean)
2	1.25	1.33	0.78	1.12
3	1.57	1.38	1.34	1.43
4	1.76	1.89	1.60	1.75
5	2.09	1.98	2.02	______

2. Why is it a good idea to repeat each test three times?

____

3. Which reading in the results table would you have least confidence in? Explain your answer.

____

____

4. This graph shows the first three tests. Plot the last point on the graph and complete the line.

5. How does the time it takes a paper spinner to fall depend on the length of its wings?

____

____

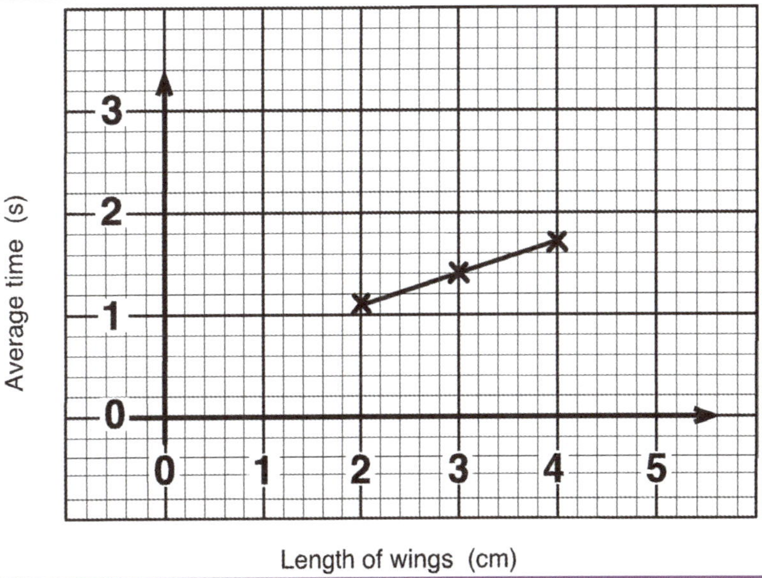

Practising my science language

1. a) Fill in the missing letters down the page to name the process in which a seed that has been dispersed begins to grow into a new seedling.

G ______________________ (plant 1)
_ ______________________ (plant 2)
_ ______________________ (plant 3)
_ ______________________ (plant 4)
I
N ______________________ (plant 5)
A ______________________ (plant 6)
T ______________________ (plant 7)
_ ______________________ (plant 8)
_ ______________________ (plant 9)
N

b) For each letter of the word in question 1(a), write the name of a plant that begins with that letter. Some of the letters are repeated. You do not have to think of another plant for these letters. You need to think of nine plants. Someone at home might be able to help you.

2. Draw lines to link the method of seed dispersal with the correct description of the seeds.

Method of seed dispersal	Description
Wind	These seeds or fruits have spiky or sticky outer shells.
Explosion	These seeds are light and sometimes fluffy.
Water	These seeds often grow in pods that dry up then suddenly split, so that the seeds shoot out.
Animal	These seeds can float and can travel large distances from the parent plant.

From school to home

Ask an adult at home to help you ...

1. **Talk to an adult about what you know about germination, and why and how plants disperse their seeds. Practise saying the key words. Say the key words in sentences.**

2. **Now ask someone at home to help you complete the following questions.**

a What did you like about this topic?

____

____

____

b What was hard to understand about this topic?

____

____

____

I understand. I understand a bit. I need more time to understand this.

3 **Now look at the checklist below. How are you doing? Circle one face for each statement.**

- I can explain why plants disperse their seeds.
- I can explain four main methods of seed dispersal: wind, explosion, animals and water.
- I can identify germination as the process that follows seed dispersal.

4 **Ask an adult at home to read and sign this.**

I have checked learning on this topic.

We have shared some understanding at home.

Signed: ______________________

Date: ______________

Teacher comment: ______________________________

____

Date: ______________

3.3 The parts of a flower, pollination and fertilisation

In Topic 3.3, you should be able to explain that plants produce flowers, which have male and female organs. You should be able to describe the main parts of a flower and their functions.

You should also be able to identify pollination as the stage after germination, and describe how insects pollinate some flowers and how seeds are formed.

1. **Why do people like getting flowers as a gift?**

   ____

   ____

2. **Why do you think flowers in a vase do not last as long as the same flowers growing in a field?**

   ____

   ____

3. **Talk to someone at home about why wild flowers are often brightly coloured and smell so sweet.**

Check your science!

1. Why do flowering plants have male parts and female parts?

   Tick the correct answer.

   ☐ To make them stronger so they are not damaged by the wind

   ☐ To share nutrients needed for healthy growth

   ☐ To allow them to reproduce and make new plants

   ☐ To make sure water gets to all parts of the plant

2. Label this lily. Use the words in the box:

   stamen carpel petal

3. Insects transfer tiny grains of pollen from one plant to another.

   What do we call this process? ____________________

4. Which process happens after the transfer of pollen but before a new seed forms?

   ____

Practising my science language

1. Here are the answers to some questions. For each one, write an example of a question you could ask that would have this answer. An example has been given.

a) Answer: Petals

Question: What is the name of the brightly coloured parts of the plant?

b) Answer: Insects

Question: ______________________________

c) Answer: Because insects like bright colours

Question: ______________________________

d) Answer: Nectar

Question: ______________________________

Practising my science language

2. Complete the crossword using these key words:

stamen sepals carpel petals pollen fertilisation female

Across

2. At the centre of a flower, made up of the stigma, style and ovary.
6. The process during which pollen and female egg cell meet.
7. These are brightly coloured to attract insects to a flower.

Down

1. These protect a flower's petals in its buds.
3. The carpel contains the __________ organs in a flower.
4. This male part of a flower is where pollen is made.
5. The tiny grains that get transferred to other flowers, often by insects.

From school to home

Ask an adult at home to help you ...

1. Talk to an adult about what you know about the parts of a flower, pollination and fertilisation. Practise saying the key words. Say the key words in sentences.

2. Now ask someone at home to help you complete the following questions.

a What did you like about this topic?

____

____

____

b What was hard to understand about this topic?

____

____

____

I understand.

I understand a bit.

I need more time to understand this.

3 **Now look at the checklist below. How are you doing? Circle one face for each statement.**

- I know that plants produce flowers that have male and female organs.
- I can label the main parts of a flower.
- I know what the main parts of a flower do.
- I can identify pollination as the next stage after germination.
- I can describe how insects pollinate some flowers.
- I know how seeds are formed.

4 **Ask an adult at home to read and sign this.**

I have checked learning on this topic.

We have shared some understanding at home.

Signed: ______________________________

Date: __________________

Teacher comment: ______________________________________

____

Date: __________________

3.4 Life cycles of flowering plants

In Topic 3.4, you should be able to describe the life cycle of a flowering plant, including the processes of:

- pollination
- fertilisation
- seed production
- seed dispersal
- germination.

Salim the seed has a time machine. He travels forwards in time to see what will happen to him during the life cycle of a flowering plant.

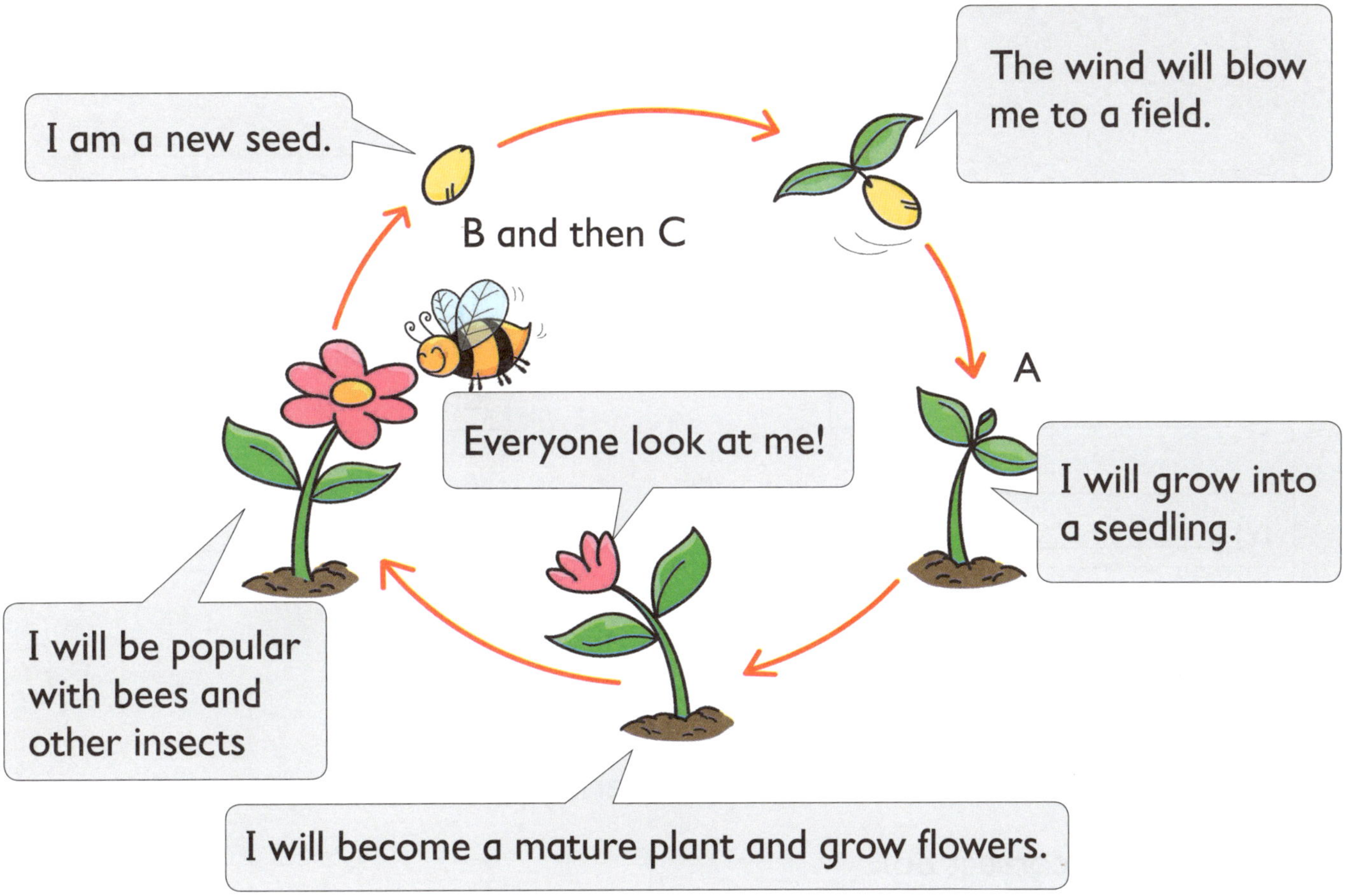

1. Which process in the life cycle happens at:

A? ______________________________

B? ______________________________

C? ______________________________

2. Explain what is happening in Salim's life cycle to someone at home.

Check your science!

1. Fill in the missing words to complete these sentences:

a) All living things have a life ____________________.

b) This includes stages of ____________________ as the living thing gets bigger and always involves some kind of ____________________ (the making of new individuals).

2. a) Fill in the missing letters in this life cycle of a flowering plant. The first letter of each missing word is given:

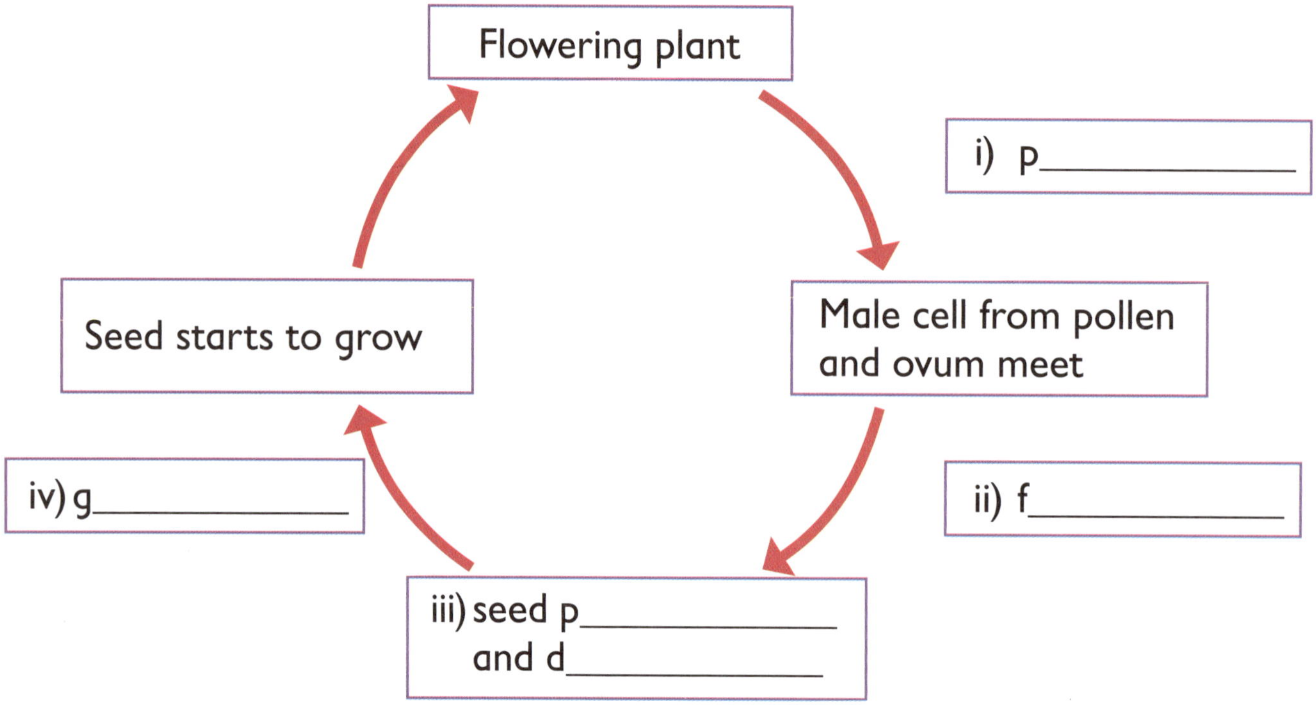

b) Where is the seed formed in a flowering plant?

Tick the correct box.

- ☐ In the stamen
- ☐ In the ovary
- ☐ In the style
- ☐ On the stigma

c) Why do you think that plants make lots of seeds?

____

Practising my
science language

1. Draw lines to match each process to its definition.

Process	Definition
Pollination	The process by which the seed starts to grow.
Fertilisation	The process in which the ovum develops into a seed and the ovary develops into a fruit.
Seed production	The process by which pollen fertilises the ovum.
Seed dispersal	The process by which pollen is transferred from the male part of a flower to the female part of a flower, often by insects.
Germination	The process by which the seedling grows into a young plant, and then a mature plant that is capable of flowering.
Growth	The process by which seeds are released and spread from the plant. This can be by wind, explosion, animals or water.

Practising my

science language

2. Find these words in the wordsearch.

seedling	growth	produce	seed
germination	flower	disperse	pollen

t	s	e	e	d	l	i	n	g	g	e	e	t	e
g	o	p	n	c	s	t	t	g	f	i	e	o	g
u	e	i	r	g	i	n	p	e	d	h	e	d	n
n	w	r	w	o	f	e	d	n	i	e	e	e	l
e	l	n	m	d	d	e	s	e	f	s	r	p	l
s	p	l	d	i	o	u	r	e	e	e	n	o	w
r	o	i	e	s	n	i	c	s	e	l	u	o	s
e	l	n	t	g	t	a	s	e	n	s	r	l	o
p	l	r	m	o	n	n	t	f	l	o	w	e	r
s	e	h	t	w	o	r	g	i	i	g	l	g	g
i	n	p	o	l	u	t	p	d	o	w	e	o	r
d	o	i	p	i	d	i	u	e	r	n	f	o	i
i	g	o	l	n	r	p	l	e	i	o	o	l	r
g	d	w	r	l	d	s	n	s	u	w	d	e	a

From school to home

Ask an adult at home to help you ...

1. Talk to an adult about what you know about the life cycle of a flowering plant. Practise saying the key words. Say the key words in sentences.

2. Now ask someone at home to help you complete the following questions.

a What did you like about this topic?

____

____

____

b What was hard to understand about this topic?

____

____

____

I understand.

I understand a bit.

I need more time to understand this.

3 **Now look at the checklist below. How are you doing? Circle one face for each statement.**

- I know that flowering plants have a life cycle.
- I know that their life cycle includes pollination, fertilisation, seed production, seed dispersal and germination.
- I can construct the life cycle of a flowering plant.

4 **Ask an adult at home to read and sign this.**

I have checked learning on this topic.

We have shared some understanding at home.

Signed: ______________________

Date: ______________

Teacher comment: ______________________________

____

Date: ______________

4 Investigating plant growth

4.1 Investigating germination

In Topic 4.1, you should be able to investigate the conditions that are needed for seeds to germinate.

This will include predicting, planning, carrying out and evaluating your own investigation.

Picture 1

Picture 2

1. Look at picture 1. What do you think of Malik's dad's idea about seeds in the dark? Explain your answer.

____

____

2. Look at picture 2. What do you think of Malik's dad's idea about seeds and water? Explain your answer.

____

____

Check your science!

1. Tick the correct boxes to show the three things seeds need to germinate.

☐ soil	☐ water	☐ warm temperatures
☐ low temperatures	☐ air	☐ fertiliser

2. A class are investigating germination.
   - Group **A** investigate the effect of light or dark, in cold conditions.
   - Group **B** investigate the effect of light or dark, in warm conditions.
   - Group **C** investigate the effect of warm or cold conditions, in the light.
   - Group **D** investigate the effect of warm or cold conditions, in the dark.

   a) Describe how Group **D** could set up their investigation using cress seeds on moist cotton wool in two shallow dishes. They have a fridge available.

   ____

   ____

   b) Group **C** have the same equipment and seeds as Group **D**. They also have a fridge available.
   Why is Group **C**'s investigation more difficult to set up than Group **D**'s investigation?

   ____

   ____

   c) Group **A** did their investigation. They found that no cress seeds germinated.
   Group **B** found that both their dishes have cress seeds that germinated.
   What can Group **A** and **B** conclude from their two sets of results?

   ____

   ____

   d) If Groups **A** and **B** are correct, predict how many dishes Groups **C** and **D** would find had germinated seeds. Circle your answer.

Group C:	**0 dishes**	**1 dish**	**2 dishes**
Group D:	**0 dishes**	**1 dish**	**2 dishes**

Practising my
science language

1. Draw lines to link each question you must answer in an investigation to the correct stage of the investigation.

Question	Stage in investigation
What do you think will happen in your investigation?	Results
How will you carry out your investigation?	Conclusion
What happened in your investigation?	Prediction
What did you find out in your investigation?	Evaluation
How could you improve your investigation?	Plan/Method

Practising my science language

Hakim and Rana investigated whether or not water is needed for seeds to germinate. Read their plan:

We will use two round dishes with the same amount of cotton wool in each one.

In the first dish, we will keep the cotton wool damp with water.

We will leave the cotton wool in the second dish dry (without water).

Then we will add one cress seed to each dish and check which seed germinates when they are kept in the same place.

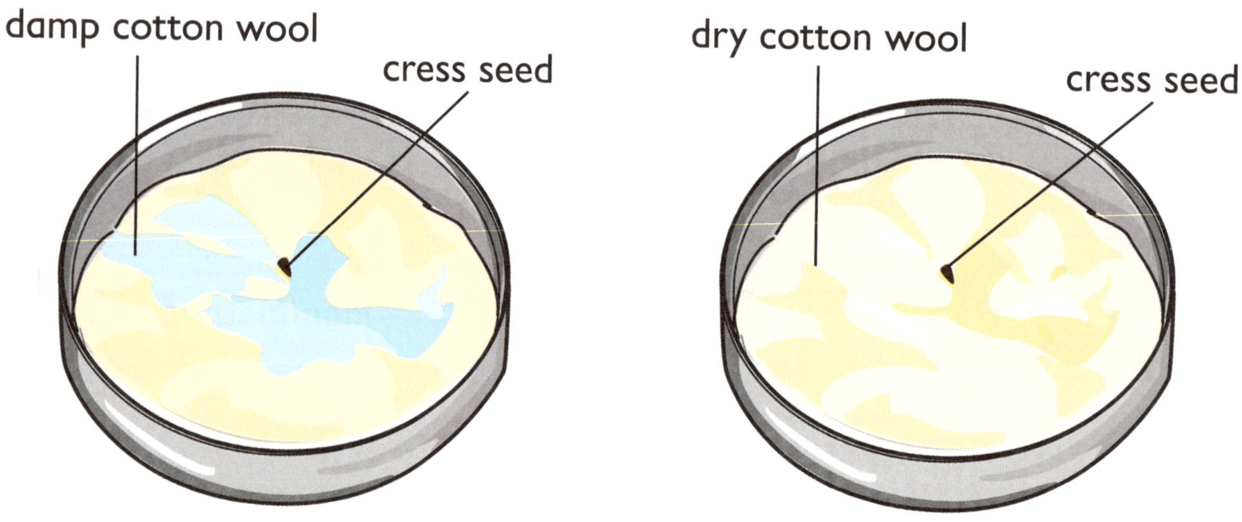

first dish

second dish

2. Circle the correct answer to complete the sentences:

a) Hakim and Rana kept the dishes in the same place to make sure their investigation was **a fair test / reliable**.

b) Rana was thinking about their investigation. She said to Hakim, "I really think we should use more than one seed in each dish if we want our results to be **a fair test / reliable**."

From school to home

Ask an adult at home to help you ...

1. Talk to an adult about what you know about investigating germination. Practise saying the key words. Say the key words in sentences.

2. Now ask someone at home to help you complete the following questions.

a What did you like about this topic?

____

____

____

b What was hard to understand about this topic?

____

____

____

I understand. I understand a bit. I need more time to understand this.

3 **Now look at the checklist below. How are you doing? Circle one face for each statement.**

- I can plan an investigation into the germination of seeds.
- I can make a prediction about germination using my scientific knowledge.
- I can carry out an investigation about germination and draw conclusions from the results.
- I can evaluate an investigation into germination.

4 **Ask an adult at home to read and sign this.**

I have checked learning on this topic.

We have shared some understanding at home.

Signed: ______________________

Date: ______________

Teacher comment: ______________________________

____

Date: ______________

4.2 Investigating plant growth and the energy it needs

In Topic 4.2, you should be able to investigate how a factor, such as light, affects plant growth. You should also understand that plants get energy from light to grow.

Malik's dad planted some seeds in his greenhouse. They germinated and have now started growing into mature plants. But he is getting impatient. He wants the plants to grow faster!

1. Explain why Malik's dad has the wrong idea about plant growth.

____

____

____

2. Show your answer to question 1 to someone at home. What advice would you give Malik's dad to help make his greenhouse plants grow well?

____

____

____

Check your science!

1. Tick the correct boxes to show the three things plants need to grow well.

- [ ] salt
- [ ] water
- [ ] darkness
- [ ] carbon dioxide gas
- [ ] light energy
- [ ] cotton wool

2. Complete the diagram of the plant to show the three things plants need to grow.

   You can draw new things, and add arrows and labels.

Practising my science language

1. Fill in the missing letters to complete the answers next to each clue. Some of the letters are given:

   a) Plants get their light energy from this. the _ _ _

   b) Plants use this gas from the air.

   c _ _ _ _ _ d _ _ _ _ _ _

   c) A plant's roots absorb this from the soil. w _ _ _ _

   d) Plants will not grow well if they are kept in this. _ _ _ k

   e) What word is made in the vertical box? _ _ _ _

2. Deshi and Anka measured the height of a plant every two days and recorded their results. Unfortunately their results got mixed up.

   a) Complete the headings in the table.

   b) Sort the results into the correct order and add them to the table.

   After 4 days the plant was 21 mm high.

   After 8 days the plant was 35 mm high.

   After 0 days the plant was 12 mm high.

   After 6 days the plant was 29 mm high.

   After 2 days the plant was 17 mm high.

Time in d _ _ _	H _ _ _ _ _ of plant in mm

From school to home

Ask an adult at home to help you ...

1. Talk to an adult about what you know about factors that affect plant growth, and how plants need energy to grow. Practise saying the key words. Say the key words in sentences.

2. Now ask someone at home to help you complete the following questions.

a What did you like about this topic?

____

____

____

b What was hard to understand about this topic?

____

____

____

I understand. I understand a bit. I need more time to understand this.

3 **Now look at the checklist below. How are you doing? Circle one face for each statement.**

- I know what green plants need to grow.
- I can plan an investigation into a factor (such as light) that affects plant growth.
- I can carry out my investigation into plant growth and draw a graph to display the results.
- I can draw conclusions and evaluate my investigation into plant growth.

4 **Ask an adult at home to read and sign this.**

I have checked learning on this topic.

We have shared some understanding at home.

Signed: ____________________

Date: ____________

Teacher comment: ____________________________

____

Date: ____________

5 Earth's movements

5.1 The apparent movement of the Sun

In Topic 5.1, you should be able to track the path of the Sun across the sky and explore how shadows are affected by the position of the Sun. You should also be able to explore sunrise and sunset times.

Hemish is walking to school with his dad one sunny morning. His dad is telling him about his visit to the doctor the day before.

1. Why is Hemish puzzled by what his dad is telling him?

____

____

____

2. If Hemish and his dad walked to school at midday, how would their shadows compare with their shadows in the morning?

____

____

Check your science!

1. a) Describe an investigation you could carry out to find out how the shadow of an object changes every hour on a sunny day.

____

____

____

____

____

____

b) A teacher plans to carry out this investigation with her class but the weather is very cloudy.

Why would she have to change her science lesson that day?

____

____

2. The table below shows data about sunrise and sunset in Moscow, Russia at different times of the year.

Date	Sun rises at ...	Sun sets at ...	Number of daylight hours
20 March	6.33	18.43	________
20 June	3.44	21.17	17.33
20 September	6.10	18.33	12.23
20 December	8.56	15.57	7.01

a) Fill in the missing data for 20 March.

b) In which month does the Sun rise earliest in the day? ____________

c) In which month does the Sun set latest in the day? ____________

d) In which month is the data collected in the winter? ____________

e) In which month would you expect the Sun to reach its highest position in the sky? ____________

Practising my science language

Brianna writes and draws in her science book:

1. One of Brianna's sentences is correct and one is incorrect.

Write Brianna's correct sentence.

____

2. Fill in the missing letters to correct Brianna's incorrect sentence.

The Sun moves a _ _ _ _ s the sky, rising to a peak around mid _ _ _.

3. Draw your own picture to show how the Sun appears to move in the sky.

Label the Sun at sunrise, sunset and midday.

From school to home

Ask an adult at home to help you ...

1. Talk to an adult about what you know about the apparent movement of the Sun in the sky during the day and how this affects shadows. Practise saying the key words. Say the key words in sentences.

2. Now ask someone at home to help you complete the following questions.

a What did you like about this topic?

____

____

____

b What was hard to understand about this topic?

____

____

____

I understand. | I understand a bit. | I need more time to understand this.

3 Now look at the checklist below. How are you doing? Circle one face for each statement.

- I can track the path of the Sun across the sky.
- I understand how shadows are affected by the position of the Sun.
- I can explore sunrise and sunset times.

4 **Ask an adult at home to read and sign this.**

I have checked learning on this topic.

We have shared some understanding at home.

Signed: ______________________

Date: ______________

Teacher comment: ______________________________

____

Date: ______________

5.2 The spinning and orbiting Earth

In Topic 5.2, you should be able to model the movement of the Earth and Sun to explain day and night. You should understand that the Sun does not move around the Earth and that the Sun appears to move because the Earth is spinning on its axis.

You should also be able to model the movement of the Earth and Sun to explain the length of a year and explain that the Earth orbiting the Sun causes our different seasons.

Rasheed is trying to explain how the Earth moves to his younger sister. He models the Earth and its movement while his little sister models the Sun.

1. **Explain how Rasheed is moving while demonstrating his model of the Earth and the Sun to his sister.**

____

____

____

2. **Show your answer to someone at home and try the model yourselves!**

Check your science!

1. Josue thinks that when it is night-time where he lives, it is night-time everywhere on the Earth.

   Explain why Josue is wrong.

   ____

   ____

   ____

2. a) Place the Earth, Moon and Sun in order of size:

   i) (biggest) ____________

   ii) ____________

   iii) (smallest) ____________

   b) Which one of these statements is correct?

   Tick the correct answer.

   ☐ The Sun moves closer to the Earth in summer.

   ☐ Daytime is shorter than night-time in summer compared to winter.

   ☐ It takes longer for the Earth to travel once around the Sun than for the Earth to spin around once.

3. a) How long does it take for the Earth to orbit the Sun? ____________

   b) How long does it take for the Earth to spin around once on its own axis?

   ____

4. Which one of the following causes the different seasons on Earth?

   Tick the correct answer.

   ☐ The speed at which the Earth spins

   ☐ The distance between the Earth and the Moon

   ☐ The tilt of the Earth's axis

   ☐ The energy released from the Sun

Practising my
science language

1. Unscramble the letters to find the names of the eight planets.

Name of planet

a) S R A M _ _ _ _

b) U T P E N E N _ _ _ _ _ _ _

c) U V N E S _ _ _ _ _

d) R Y M C U E R _ _ _ _ _ _ _

e) E R P U I T J _ _ _ _ _ _ _

f) T A H E R _ _ _ _ _

g) A N S R U T _ _ _ _ _ _

h) N U A S R U _ _ _ _ _ _

2. Put the following lengths of time in order:

hour week minute year second month day

a) (shortest) ____________

b) ____________

c) ____________

d) ____________

e) ____________

f) ____________

g) (longest) ____________

3. Explain the movement of the Earth to someone at home.
Use these key words and phrases:

Earth 24 hours spin travel space
orbit the Sun one year

From school to home

Ask an adult at home to help you ...

1. **Talk to an adult about what you know about how the movement of the Earth and Sun explains night and day, the length of a year and the seasons. Practise saying the key words. Say the key words in sentences.**

2. **Now ask someone at home to help you complete the following questions.**

a What did you like about this topic?

____

____

____

b What was hard to understand about this topic?

____

____

____

I understand. | I understand a bit. | I need more time to understand this.

3 **Now look at the checklist below. How are you doing? Circle one face for each statement.**

- I can model the movement of the Earth and Sun to explain night and day.
- I know that the Sun does not move around the Earth.
- I know that the Sun appears to move because the Earth is spinning on its axis.
- I can model the movement of the Earth and Sun to explain the length of a year.
- I know that the Earth orbiting the Sun causes our different seasons.

4 **Ask an adult at home to read and sign this.**

I have checked learning on this topic.

We have shared some understanding at home.

Signed: ______________________

Date: ______________

Teacher comment: ______________________________

____

Date: ______________

5.3 Space science

In Topic 5.3, you should understand the different approaches scientists (including space scientists) can take to answer their questions.

You should also be able to carry out research into the life and discoveries of a space scientist, and to develop scientific enquiry skills while investigating craters.

1. Explain how the darker patches on the Moon were probably formed.

____

____

____

2. Share your ideas with someone at home.

Check your science!

Chad and Jessica investigate how the size of the craters formed in sand is affected by the speed at which an object hits the surface. They decide to:

- use a ball of modelling clay (wrapped in cling film) as the object to drop
- change the height from which they drop the ball of clay (to change its speed) and repeat the test three times at each height
- measure the diameter of the crater made in the damp sand.

1. Suggest why:

a) they wrapped the clay in cling film. ______________________________

____

b) they made the sand damp. ______________________________

____

c) they repeated each test three times. ______________________________

____

2. Here is the table of their results:

Height ball is dropped from in cm	Diameter of crater in cm			
	1st try	2nd try	3rd try	Average
2	3.2	3.3	3.1	________
4	3.7	3.7	3.7	________
6	4.0	4.0	4.6	________
8	4.3	4.2	4.4	________
10	4.5	4.7	4.6	________

a) Work out the five averages and complete the table.

b) At which height were the results most reliable? ____________ cm

c) What pattern can you see in the average diameter?

As the speed of the ball increases, the diameter of the crater

____________________.

3. Chad and Jessica plan to draw a graph to display their results.

What type of graph will they use? Tick the correct answer.

☐ **Bar chart** ☐ **Line graph**

Practising my

science language

1. We use many different approaches to find the answers to scientific questions.

   Think about the Sun. Write down a question you could investigate for each of these question-words. An example for the first question has been given:

   a) **Where** does the sun rise and set each day?

   b) **Why** ____

   ____?

   c) **What** ____

   ____?

   d) **When** ____

   ____?

   e) **Which** ____

   ____?

   f) **Who** ____?

2. Look at this graph:

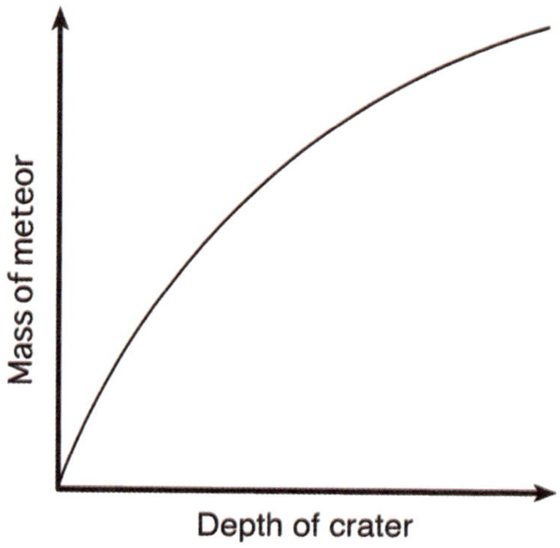

   a) Fill in the missing word to complete the question that is being investigated:

      How does the mass of a meteor affect the ____________________ of the crater it forms?

   b) Fill in the missing word to complete the pattern shown by the line on the graph:

      The greater the mass of the meteor, the ____________________ the crater.

From school to home

Ask an adult at home to help you ...

1. Talk to an adult about what you know about the different approaches scientists (including space scientists) can take to answer their questions. Tell them about the life and discoveries of one particular space scientist. Practise saying the key words. Say the key words in sentences.

2. Now ask someone at home to help you complete the following questions.

a What did you like about this topic?

____

____

____

b What was hard to understand about this topic?

____

____

____

I understand. I understand a bit. I need more time to understand this.

3 **Now look at the checklist below. How are you doing? Circle one face for each statement.**

- I know about the different approaches scientists (including space scientists) can take to answer questions.
- I have researched the life and discoveries of a space scientist.
- I have investigated the size of craters on the Moon and:
  - I understand the need for repeated measurements
  - I can present results in tables, bar charts and/or line graphs
  - I can decide whether results support predictions and evaluate repeated results.

4 **Ask an adult at home to read and sign this.**

I have checked learning on this topic.

We have shared some understanding at home.

Signed: ______________________

Date: ______________

Teacher comment: ______________________________

____

Date: ______________

6 Shadows

6.1 How do shadows form?

In Topic 6.1, you should be able to observe and explain how shadows are formed. You should also be able to explain shadows using the idea of rays of light.

Dev is giving a shadow puppet show to his younger brother.

Dev's brother asks him why the "crocodile" is bigger than Dev's hands.

How could Dev explain what is happening to his brother?

____

____

____

____

____

Check your science!

1. a) Describe how you would show a ray of light on a science diagram.

____

____

____

b) Tick the diagram that will make the biggest shadow on the wall.

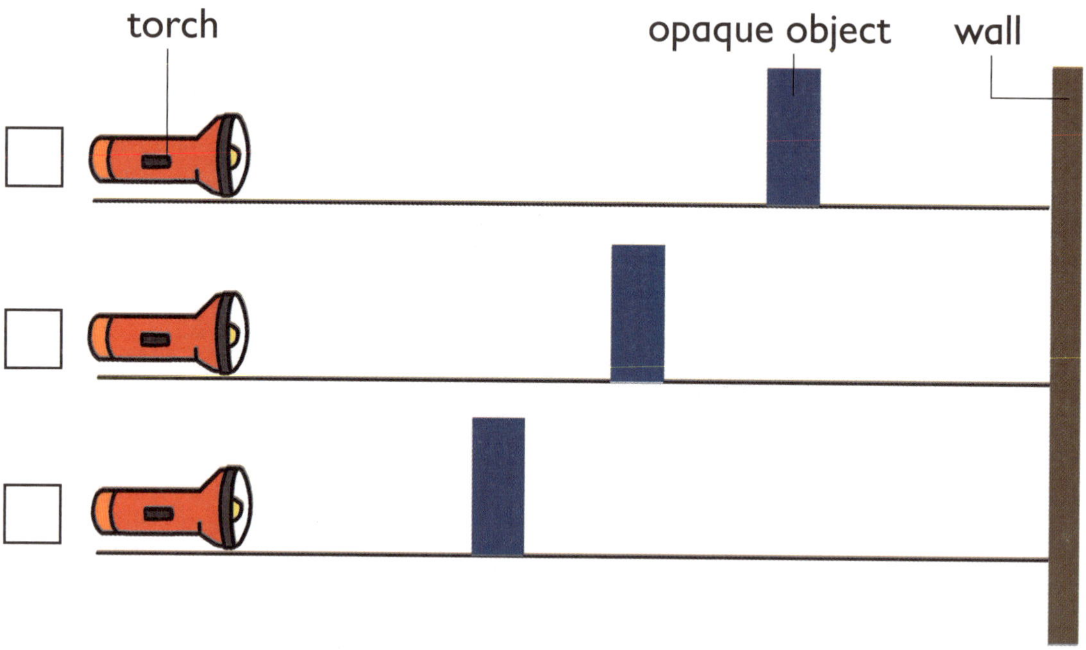

2. Fill in the missing words to complete these sentences. Use the words from this list:

darker blocks edges source

a) When an object ______________ the light rays hitting it, the area of darkness formed is the object's shadow.

b) Shadows form "behind" objects, opposite the light ______________.

c) The brighter the light hitting the object, the ______________ the shadow appears.

d) Shadows are not always sharp, black areas with clear ______________.

Practising my

science language

1. Rearrange the letters to find a key word for this topic. Two of the letters are already in place.

   Clue: Think about the shadow puppet show.

   i h o t e e u t

   s __ l __ __ __ __ __ __ __

2. Fill in the missing letters to complete this sentence about light:

   Light always travels in __ __ __ __ __ __ __ __ lines.

3. You may have made a shadow puppet and put on your own shadow puppet show. If so:

   a) describe how you made your puppet

   ____

   ____

   b) describe the story of your puppet show.

   ____

   ____

   ____

   ____

   ____

   ____

From school to home

Ask an adult at home to help you ...

1. Talk to an adult about what you know about how shadows are formed. Practise saying the key words. Say the key words in sentences.

2. Now ask someone at home to help you complete the following questions.

a What did you like about this topic?

____

____

____

b What was hard to understand about this topic?

____

____

____

I understand. I understand a bit. I need more time to understand this.

3 **Now look at the checklist below. How are you doing? Circle one face for each statement.**

- I know that shadows are formed when light travelling from a source is blocked.
- I can observe and explain how shadows are formed.
- I can explain shadows using the idea of rays of light.

4 **Ask an adult at home to read and sign this.**

I have checked learning on this topic.

We have shared some understanding at home.

Signed: ______________________

Date: ______________

Teacher comment: ____________________________

____

Date: ______________

6.2 Opaque, translucent and transparent materials

In Topic 6.2, you should be able to explain the meaning of the terms "opaque", "translucent" and "transparent". You should also be able to investigate how to classify materials as opaque, translucent or transparent.

Tomi is taking a shower. It is daytime – so the bathroom is light – but people cannot see him clearly.

Inside Tomi's bathroom

Outside Tomi's bathroom

1. **Explain how Tomi's window lets light in but only shows a blurred image of Tomi from the outside.**

___

___

___

2. **Show your answer to someone at home. Explain to them what is happening to the light.**

Check your science!

1. What is the difference between transparent objects, translucent objects and opaque objects?

   Complete the sentences below:

   a) Transparent objects ______________________________.

   b) Translucent objects ______________________________.

   c) Opaque objects ______________________________.

2. In the table, write two materials that are transparent, two that are translucent and two that are opaque.

Transparent	Translucent	Opaque

3. Using a pencil and a ruler, continue the rays of light to show the path they will take as they carry on towards the objects.

transparent block

opaque block

translucent block

Practising my science language

1. Put the following materials into the correct column in the table.

wood air stone steel water
copper frosted glass tissue paper glass

Transparent	Translucent	Opaque

2. Describe an investigation you could do to classify objects as transparent, translucent or opaque. Include a diagram.

From school to home

Ask an adult at home to help you ...

1 Talk to an adult about what you know about opaque, transparent and translucent materials. Practise saying the key words. Say the key words in sentences.

2 Now ask someone at home to help you complete the following questions.

a What did you like about this topic?

____

____

____

b What was hard to understand about this topic?

____

____

____

I understand.

I understand a bit.

I need more time to understand this.

3 **Now look at the checklist below. How are you doing? Circle one face for each statement.**

- I know the meaning of the terms opaque, translucent and transparent.
- I can investigate how to classify materials as opaque, translucent or transparent.

4 **Ask an adult at home to read and sign this.**

I have checked learning on this topic.

We have shared some understanding at home.

Signed: ____________________

Date: ____________

Teacher comment: __________________________

____

Date: ____________

6.3 Factors affecting shadows

In Topic 6.3, you should be able to investigate how the size of a shadow is affected by the position of the object. You should understand how shadows change in length and position throughout the day.

You should also be able to describe how we can use the Sun to tell the time and how to make a sundial.

1. Explain some of the problems with a sundial wristwatch. Why would it not work?

____

____

____

2. Share your ideas with someone at home.

Check your science!

Jared and Hana investigated how the distance between a torch and a pencil affected the size of the pencil's shadow. They decided to:

- change the distance between the torch and the pencil by moving the torch
- keep the pencil in the same place
- measure the height of the pencil's shadow on a wall.

1. Write down one thing they did to make the test fair. ____________________

____

2. Here is a table of their results:

Distance between torch and pencil in cm	Height of shadow in cm
5	55
10	44
15	16
20	10
25	8

What pattern can you see in the table? Fill in the missing word:

As the distance between the torch and the pencil increases, the height of the pencil's shadow ____________________.

3. Jared and Hana plan to draw a graph to display their results. What type of graph will they use? Tick the correct answer.

☐ **Bar chart** ☐ **Line graph**

4. Another group did the same investigation. They put the pencil the same distance from the wall as in Jared and Hana's investigation. They also carried out tests with 5 cm, 10 cm, 15 cm, 20 cm and 25 cm between the torch and the pencil.

They found the same pattern but their shadows were all shorter than in Jared and Hana's results. Suggest why their shadows were shorter.

____

5. The other group did an extra test with a distance of 30 cm between the torch and the pencil. The pencil's shadow was 11 cm high.

What do you suggest the group should do with this extra result?

____

Practising my

science language

1. What do we call an instrument that tells us the time using the position of the Sun in the sky? _ _ _ _ _ _ _

2. A group carried out an investigation using a torch, a pencil and a ruler.

This is the graph of their results:

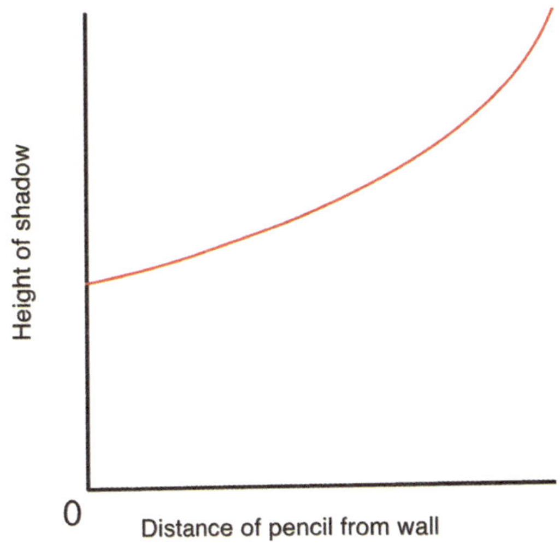

a) Fill in the missing words to complete the question they were investigating:

How does the ______________ of a pencil from a wall affect the ______________ of the shadow formed?

b) In the investigation, the light source was kept in the same position.

Fill in the missing word to complete the pattern shown by the line on the graph.

The greater the distance of the pencil from the wall, the ______________ the shadow gets.

c) Predict how the line on the graph would change if a smaller pencil was used in the investigation.

The line on the graph would ______________________________
____.

d) The group had a choice of two torches to use in their investigation. Both torches had bulbs of the same brightness, but one had a wider opening for the light to come out of.

Tick the torch that would give a sharper shadow to measure.

☐  ☐ 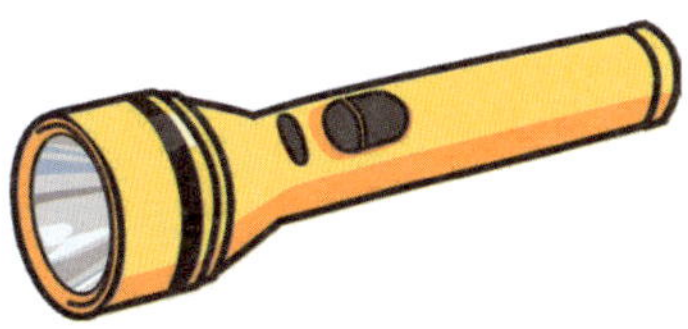

From school to home

Ask an adult at home to help you …

1. Talk to an adult about what you know about factors that can affect the size of a shadow, and about how and why shadows change throughout the day. Practise saying the key words. Say the key words in sentences.

2. Now ask someone at home to help you complete the following questions.

a What did you like about this topic?

____

____

____

b What was hard to understand about this topic?

____

____

____

I understand. I understand a bit. I need more time to understand this.

3 **Now look at the checklist below. How are you doing? Circle one face for each statement.**

- I can investigate how the size of a shadow is affected by the position of the object, including:
  - I can make and explain predictions of what will happen
  - I can plan how to carry out a fair test
  - I can draw a graph of my results
  - I can collect enough evidence to test my ideas.
- I know how shadows change in length throughout the day.
- I know how shadows change position throughout the day.
- I can use the Sun to tell the time.
- I can make a sundial.

4 **Ask an adult at home to read and sign this.**

I have checked learning on this topic.

We have shared some understanding at home.

Signed: ______________________

Date: ______________

Teacher comment: ______________________________

____

Date: ______________

6.4 How bright is it?

In Topic 6.4, you should understand that the brightness of light in a place is called the light intensity, and know how light intensity can be measured and investigated.

You should also know where it is important to measure light intensity.

1. **Explain how a cricket umpire judges whether light conditions are too low to continue with the game.**

____

____

____

2. **Share your ideas with someone at home. Do they know why a team might choose to play on if they only use slow bowlers until the conditions get lighter?**

Check your science!

A teacher monitored the light intensity in a classroom. She left a data-logging light meter at the front of the room for 24 hours. Here is a graph of her results:

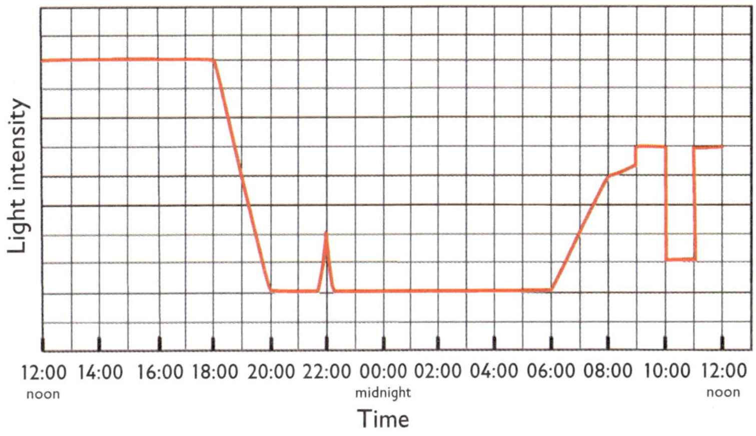

1. What time did the teacher start her monitoring experiment? ____________

2. a) Which day was brighter?

   Tick the correct answer.

   ☐ The day the experiment started

   ☐ The day the experiment finished

   b) How can you tell?

   ____

3. a) What time was sunset? ____________________

   b) What time was sunrise? ____________________

4. The school caretaker checked the classrooms before locking up. What time did he carry out his check in the teacher's classroom?

   ____

5. a) What time did the teacher arrive in the classroom on the second day? ____________________

   b) Explain your answer.

   ____

6. The class did an experiment using torches to look at shadows.

   a) When did they start their experiment? ____________________

   b) How long did the experiment last? ____________________

7. Give one advantage of using data-logging in science experiments, like the one carried out by the teacher.

   ____

Practising my

science language

1. a) What do we call an instrument that measures the brightness of light?

   _ _ _ _ _   _ _ _ _ _

   b) Fill in the missing word to complete the sentence. The first letter of the word is given:

   We say that this instrument measures the i_ _ _ _ _ _ _ _ of light.

2. A group plans to investigate how the number of pieces of tissue paper affects the brightness of the light that can pass through.

   a) Which variable would they **change** in each test?

   Fill in the missing word to complete the sentence.

   The number of _ _ _ _ _ _ of tissue paper.

   b) i) Which variable would they **measure** to judge the effect of changing the variable in question 2(a)?

   ____

   ii) What would they use to measure this variable?

   ____

   c) Draw a line on the graph to predict their results.

   d) Fill in the missing word to complete the pattern shown by the line on the graph:

   The more pieces of paper the light has to pass through, the ____________________ light that gets through.

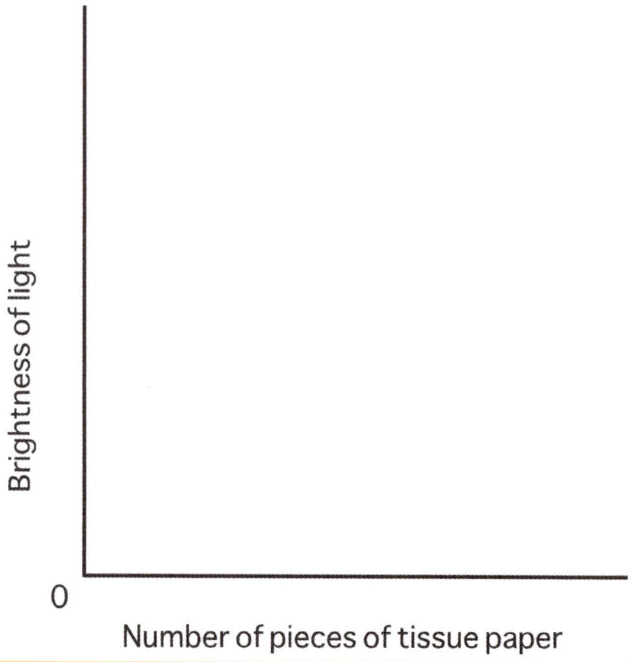

From school to home

Ask an adult at home to help you ...

1. Talk to an adult about what you know about light intensity, and how it is measured and investigated. Practise saying the key words. Say the key words in sentences.

2. Now ask someone at home to help you complete the following questions.

a What did you like about this topic?

____

____

____

b What was hard to understand about this topic?

____

____

____

I understand. I understand a bit. I need more time to understand this.

3 **Now look at the checklist below. How are you doing? Circle one face for each statement.**

- I know that the brightness of light in a place is called the light intensity.
- I know that light intensity can be measured.
- I can describe some places where it is important to measure light intensity.

4 **Ask an adult at home to read and sign this.**

I have checked learning on this topic.

We have shared some understanding at home.

Signed: ______________________

Date: ______________

Teacher comment: ______________________________

____

Date: ______________